MY LOVER'S DISCOURSE

My Lover's Discourse

BK Fischer

TINDERBOX
EDITIONS

Tinderbox Editions
Molly Sutton Kiefer, Publisher and Editor
Red Wing, Minnesota
tinderboxeditions@gmail.com
www.tinderboxeditions.org

Cover art and design by Nikkita Cohoon
Interior design by Nikkita Cohoon
Author photo by Gina DeCaprio Vercesi

for Emily, in 2044

Contents

My Lover's Discourse

MY LOVER'S DISCOURSE

The necessity for this book is found in the following consideration: the lover's discourse is today not an *extreme solitude* but an *extreme plenitude*.

Roland Barthes's *A Lover's Discourse* becomes a sacred text because it inhabits our intimacy, seeps into the cellular spaces of our erotic thinking. It has our number, dials us up, indulges our agony, then hangs up on us and hangs us up, weeping, to dry.

It is ripe for a redo—taken on a slant that is not male, French, or esoteric, but female, American, and tacky. Taken to the mat, taken to the cleaners, taken from behind. This is what I want: a gorgeous mess. Not soliloquy but colloquy, collusion between ripeness and rot, pillow talk between doze and decompose. This discourse too is spoken by *thousands of subjects*, by men and women, *but warranted by no one*: it is fulcrum, foam-at-the-mouth, meniscus, hangnail, hinge. The knotted under-tapestry. The fuse box, the figuring out which one is blown. The verso, the thread hanging off an old nightgown.

My lover's discourse picks up things Barthes left lying around: ransom, ricochet, the *faint murmur of draining bathtubs*. A cocoon. *A certain tiny stain.* A head held underwater. My lover speaks to me of amen and invective, hemlock and whiplash. *I hear a counter-rhythm: something like a syncope in the lovely phrase of the loved being, the noise of a rip in the smooth envelope.* My lover's discourse flabbergasts and capsizes, irrigates and embalms. It is not watertight. It is *the site of someone speaking within herself, amorously, confronting the other (the loved object), who does not speak.* She rants. She begs. She tergiversates about virginity, ceilings, maenads, Sappho, room service, amusement parks, and Medusa. She gets in hot water. She goes swimming.

Once a discourse is thus driven by its own momentum into the backwater, over-brimmed by its own emotion, its clammy exclamation, its incontrovertible kitsch, the prose overflows. Hence verse. The difference between prose and verse is the difference between wearing pants and wearing a dress, no more, no less. A skirt invites a breeze. *That affirmation*, American and feminine, *is, in short, the subject of the book which begins here.*

"It's a girl"

a girl / *une fille*

Only the lover and the child have a heavy heart.

Naturally the girl can do the splits both ways. *Girl* from *gyrela*, item of dress worn by girls, a metonym. We go from *female from birth* to *full growth* to *female child from birth to marriage*, so an unmarried woman, no longer a girl, is a girl. There's conjecture the Indo-European root contains *ghwrgh-*, which is also within the Greek *parthenos*, "virgin," hence *girl* equals *virgin* if we incorporate *ghwrgh-*, the ancient growl. Oh come on. Try sugar and spice. Shall we say girlie: adjective, partiality to pink. Girlie, noun, a pornographic magazine. She's your servant; she's your sweetheart. *Then spoke I to my Girle To part her lips*, to get her talking.

I don't think you were listening. Older use, usually offensive, a female employee: *a dirty slipshod girl-of-all-work*. A lass, a doll, a moppet, girl-miser, maid, coquette. Average age of menarche: 12.4 years. Average age of first kiss: 14 years. Average age of first sexual consummation: 17.3 years. Born girl: alcohol, anorexia, anxiety, beer, bullying, cutting class, cutting flesh, cyber addiction, cyber bullying, depression, driving under the influence, inhalants, kidnapping, overdose, predators, prescription drugs, sexting, smoking, STDs, stress, study drugs, tanning, teen pregnancy, texting while driving, tobacco, truancy. LIFE magazine, referring to Doris Day: *she's the girl next door, all right—next door to the bank.*

To think of a gal o' your age wanting to go and sit with half-a-dozen men! Did you not think you would find me in my father's house?

Lyrics

ardor / *ardeur*

Dis-cursus—originally the action of running here and there, comings and goings, measures taken, "plots and plans": the lover, in fact, cannot keep her mind from racing.

She tries to lose herself
on a muddy path where

skunk cabbages erupt
from winter mire, birches

green with green so new
it can't be natural. A few

bars into the third song—
a guileless chime, some

moody business with
a flute from the get-go,

bits of baroque guitar
sidling up like the cringe

of existing at 17 in skin
aflame at the touch of air—

that's desire. As she
rounds the next bend

of the brook it strums
and whistles through

an interior ocean's rocking
of long, capricious fugues

and chorals, through
mistywet, ferryboat, slip-

stream, cherrywine—
words she wants to

pick up to skip them
across the lake. Miles

later she hears the same
song coming down the far

side of Eagle Hill under
ashen granite, and

that's when she loses
track of her body and it

feels like flying.

"Apology"

atonement / *expiation*

The girl tries to explain.

Makeshift, a poor specimen: she wore a sad apology for a hat. She didn't mean it. She had just gotten her driver's license and was thinking about a boy when she shifted into reverse—her arm thrown over the seat the way he threw his arm over her shoulders, the boy she wanted to kiss, the boy with his hand in her waistband. He was always in a rush.

Split at the root: an admission of guilt and a statement in self-defense. Culpability and co-feeling. I'm sorry, but I can't. Don't. From *apo* "away" and *logia* "speech": to speak away from oneself, away-speech as boomerang, talk to the hand, remote detonation device. Caught on the prongs of two "sorries"—*I'm sorry your dog died* versus *I'm sorry I ran over your dog*—one of which leaves her in ruin, panic, as in *universal alarm*, or pregnant, as in, *full, meaningful.*

I'm sorry, but here are some apologies I couldn't write today: absent, adulterous, amok, arbitrary, auspicious. She is sorry from *sarig*, from *sore* or *wound*, hence *suffering*, hence *passion*. I'm sorry about your *passion*, regret that you have suffered thus. Now watch that word *passion* settle on its haunches in the span of centuries: from sacrificial torture, to suffering in general, to painful affliction, to fit of outrage, to strong feeling, to lust.

"Boredom"

boredom / *ennui*

The girl longs for love because she is bored out of her mind.

S he drives to the county line—Odenton spelled backwards is nuthin-tuh-do, nothing to do except grow up and leave. Turns out it's a new idea, boredom—Dickens invented it in *Bleak House* in 1852—the realm of the bore, domain of the tedious. To bore is to drill a hole, to pierce, stab, wound (see also, *passion*).

She can't stand the thought or spelling of penis in the plural. How we got from the action of drilling to a persistently annoying person is unclear, the effect of a now-forgotten anecdote. Action, stagnation, eventually a chronic malady: to weary an auditor with monotonous conversation or simply by failure to be interesting.

Bore-hole becomes perforation, aperture; augur-hole becomes *caliber*, becomes *quality*. A hole of that *caliber*. In its recesses, the Old Norse *bára*, for wave or billow, for tide. A *blue bore* is an opening in the clouds that reveals the blue sky.

Local flora

botanical / *botanique*

"She dreams a little, and she feels the dark / Encroachment
of that old catastrophe."

Sunday morning, and she wants to believe
the sea urchin spine in the pad of her toe
will absorb on its own, begin to relinquish

its sting, though it seems she's stuck with it,
the ubiquity of chagrin: moments like this,
topically antiseptic, when memory rears up

to bludgeon her with her foolishness
past and present, the precise sensation
she had as an awkward child on the cusp

of understanding why the adults laughed
when she pointed out the dildo cactus.
Loathing inheres in bathroom shag,

Epsom salts, vat of aloe vera. She could
pretend she's not the sort of person who
can tell apart frangipani and oleander,

sea rocket and purslane, not a girl whose
botanical phase was divided from her her-
petological phase by the onset of puberty.

Maywort, sea elder—she's always been good
with an index. Even the damage she is
about to do to herself and someone she loves

dissolves into the list she was once capable
of making with a straight face—cocoplum,
woolly nipple, limber caper, bugleweed,

crab pickle, bushy spurge. She hates it
when an auditor traps her in her own
erotic parody, ragged piece of sea urchin

still lodged in her toe, still pronged
at a microscopic level and hanging on
cell by cell to the spaces in her flesh,

the angle of each microscale articulated
like the pitched blades of the ceiling fan,
like the cluster of buds on the wild sage.

Fair enough, scowl at the bougainvillea—
it's the leaves that turn red, like poinsettia,
like fall. Flowers that aren't even flowers.

Tess

complexion / *teint*

"His ardor is nettled at the sight."

She clambers to her feet, her hunger
for affection long withheld, displaced
by an almost physical sense of the implacable past:

the city lies below them; that murmur
is the vociferation of its populace. She
dismounts, face bathed in the blue of The Chase,

where druidical mistletoe is still found
on aged oaks, where yew trees, not
planted by the hand of man, grow as they had grown

when they were pollarded for bows. Let
me put one kiss on those holmberry lips,
or even on that warmed cheek, and I'll stop—on my

honor, I will. She calls into the fog, jar
of treacle smashed in the basket, but no
sooner says it than she bursts into sobbing so violent

it seems to rend her. He never knew her
to be a hysterical girl by any means, and
is surprised. Vulpine slyness entwines these devices,

a reel, a round—he watches her pretty
unconscious munching through skeins
of smoke, persists with the irrelevant act of stirring

the fire: the intelligence has not yet got
to the bottom of him. He passes through
a side-wicket with trepidation, recalls nimble harts

he hunted there, green-spangled fairies
that whickered at you as you passed.
You sometimes see her twelfth year in her cheeks,

or her ninth sparkling from her eyes,
and even her fifth will flit over curves
of her mouth now and then—if she is pink, she

feels less than when pale. The baby is
carried in a wooden box with the words
Keelwell's Marmalade on the side. She sifts her mind

for a forgotten name in the debris—
Izz Huett, Retty Priddle, Car Darch,
Mercy Chant, Marian, Betsy, Liza-Lu. Marian drinks.

A thyme-scented, bird-hatching day
in May. A white muslin figure left
lying on dead leaves. Intonation, overture, appeal to

strange kin. He stumbles over roots
in the fog, calls out, but she does not
answer, resumes her walk, eyes fixed on the ground.

Regarding her daughter regarding a maenad

daughter / *fille*

She is fascinated by an image: at first shaken, electrified, stunned.

You fly right by the varnished gods,
        the tree of life and roughed-in roses,
wheat field, weathervane, and spire,
        not a second glance at the duke,
the odalisque in grisaille, the head
        of Amenhotep and all the other
colossi. You pivot on your heels,
        chassé off before I can catch
the object of your notice, the press
        of your want, before I can see
the image in your mind, your mind
        like Degas' standing mirror where
a woman preens for the Parisian milliner,
        the reflection turned away.

You cross the hall, demand to know
        how Perseus did it without getting
himself turned to stone, refuse all
        explanations involving magic
or sanctified birth, nearly knock down
        an acoustiguided matron in red
slacks on the way out of Armor,
        insist on coins for your wishes,
speculate on skull worms in several
        closed sarcophagi, and glide
right past one wiped out Christ.

Lone child, moth mind, taper
and flame, you stop short—I almost

          topple over you. You rivet,
you pearl, you freeze at this frieze—
          a dancer tilts her lean torso
to the last strains of a dying fall,
          the last maiden dancer to leave
the village walls and roam the evergreens
          with the god of ecstasy. You
close your lips over your overbite
          and stare, approve of her robe,
her miraculous strapless sandals.
          No one, not even you, has
endeavored to reshape you yet.

          Go ahead, my girl, stamp your
feet, shake off your fawn-skin cloak
          and slip into a vernal pool until
your mind has cooled—dry off in the sun,
          pick your scabs, strike the bare
earth with your fennel stalk to draw up
          lodes of milk and honey.

You put the granite in pomegranate,
          crossbow in choir—quill
of ibis, onyx, eglantine, dawn.
          Girl child, fern shade, may
this hour suffice, this day, this last
          or near-to-last hour you'll rave
and whirl your way through a world
          that's never heard of sacrifice.

"Daydream"

daydream / *rêverie*

The girl lets her mind wander.

Split: conscious unconsciousness, daylight opaque. She is everywhere warned of the taint of the unreal, of a dream indulged while awake, especially thoughts of gratified hope or ambition, rehearsals in fulfillment. Of having it her way. What's wrong with that? Walking the half mile home from the highway where the late bus let her off, she studies the streaks in the cloud-breaks and refuses to see them as on-ramps to heaven. Even the dictionary yields to cliché—a castle in the air.

Woolgathering, brown study, pie in the sky. Cognitive frivolity. Nervous consequences! Dryden, 1685: *day dreams and sickly thoughts revolving in thy breast.* Knight, 1864: *The realities of life had cured me of many day-dreams.* Scott, 1815: *We shall not pursue a lover's daydream any farther.* The girl sits daydreaming in a vignette, too busy desiring to be desirable—head in the clouds, mind in the gutter, babe in the woods.

Ceilinguistica

dream / *rêver*

Sleep returns the girl to habitats of fear.

She wakes up smothering, pinned
beneath timbers, this time the beams

of a Salem, Massachusetts, meeting-
house where they would have dunked

her in the drink. Sometimes it's girders
of low-end retail, or factory rafters,

or the pocked dropped ceiling above
the berth where she lay naked, hot,

a lover's flank blocking both fan
and light, saying restless prayers

to Our Lady of Byways. No use
trying to sleep again before the blue

seeps through the pitch. And you?
In your otherwhere, are you trying

to fall back to sleep, to fall up
through a roof that's a sieve for

the sky, a celestial hammock, or
maybe a colander to catch the errors

of the world? What do you mean
errors? What mistaken trinket,

ladder, dove? What sign, what
web, what sky, what world?

"Figure"

figure / *ligne*

So it is with the lover at grips with her figures: she struggles in a kind of lunatic sport, she spends herself, like an athlete; she "phrases," like an orator . . . . The figure is the lover at work.

Not the rhetorical but the gymnastic or choreographic sense, the ice skating sense, the spilling-out-of-the-tank-top sense, the 35-25-35 sense—she wishes, then ditches the tape measure, cinches a sack of kittens with it, clinches the debate with it, minces the transmission with it.

Underneath each figure lies a sentence, not a completed message but a *syntactical aria*. If I were you, if you were she, squinting at the subjunctive smudge, you'd see girlhood *forsaken by the surrounding languages, ignored, disparaged, or divided by them, severed not only from authority but also from the mechanisms of authority. Hers is a horizontal discourse: no transcendence, no deliverance, no novel (though a great deal of the fictive).*

She hypothesizes, demonizes, alphabetizes—to avoid, on one hand, the story, and, on the other, the wiles of pure chance. Her pure wiles. *We must not underestimate the power of chance to engender monsters.*

"Finger"

finger / *doigt*

Sacred relic, musical technique, organ of sense.

Split at the root: to caress or admire; to pinch, filch, steal. To turn about in one's fingers, to do this repeatedly or restlessly. 1611: *My little finger shall be thicker than my father's loynes.* Excuse me?

D. H. Lawrence, as usual, was on the right track, but wrong: *My body need not be fingered by the mind.* Oh but it does! Hence a *finger* is a nip of liquor, to have fingers made of lime-twigs is to be thievish, to have a finger in the pie is to be involved. Luck, blame, languor: fingers crossed, point the finger, without lifting a finger.

Sensory pedestal: rosy-fingered, finger-plum, fingerprint, finger-food, finger-paint, Finger-Lickin-Good™. To have and to hold: the ring finger is also known as the annular, leech, medical, or physic finger (the good doctor). Thus the hand words too are split at the root—handle becomes manipulate. To finger: indicate, inform, rat someone out to the police. She fingers the velvet trim: connoisseur, pickpocket.

Amtrakabashed

gaze / *regard*

*The incident is trivial (it is always trivial) but it will attract
to it whatever language I possess.*

She has a seat to herself until the train
gets crowded at Philly and the man

mutters to his kid *sit by that ugly girl
over there.* Stung, she has half a mind

to remind him she had beauty
for lunch, to whisper to the child—

ugly is beauty's aquifer, mineral silt
that feeds the creek bed before it

breaches the marsh. Not antithesis
of beauty but its ore, a thing known

not by example—wart, bent-kneed
cartwheel, gap after extraction—

but by need—prodrome, proctor,
pore—a need akin to boredom,

to chagrin, the cringe in exposure,
the sediment in the cup. She might

be uneasy before camera or corpse
but she hears the grunted age in

umbrage, bandage, salvage, spoil—
a beautiful woman looking at her image

in the mirror may very well believe the image
is herself. An ugly woman knows it is not.

Hardware

housekeeping / *ménage*

In love, she indwells.

Everyone knows no one can live
in a museum, buoyed as we are
by teal and terracotta, a coral
kimono, a hurricane lamp or
a jar of beets rendered so clear

we forget how much you want
your dark on dark, or I want
pink traces beneath moldering
browns. This is my last list poem.
I know as soon as we cross

the street and take two steps into
an urban True Value, no more
than four yards wide and stocked
to the ceiling with five of every-
thing, that we could live here, or

rather, we could make a life
from bins and pegboard racks:
vegetable peeler, key ring, four
champagne flutes, mousetraps,
power strip, gooseneck lamp.

The basement has the rest: joint
compound, copper elbows, tubs

of flux. Near the register, stuff
of a Sunday: whistle, lighter,
Silly Putty to transfer four-ink

comics from newsprint. This is
my last list in my last list poem:
you, the timbre of your voice,
your hands, which here might have
any object in them but have none.

Crush

infatuation / *engouement*

Everything signifies.

What a mess we're in: instead of a coffin,
      carve a six-foot pocket knife with
a church key & corkscrew, plant plastic ivy
      in a trough and paint a lavender man
with one sunken shoulder. Illuminate

      toaster coils & paper lanterns, mount
a trout on a yield sign, upholster a chaise
      in faux mink, & dress the mannequin
in boas & the stole of a beaded deacon.
      Hang windowpanes horizontally next

to raptors & hinged globes made of license
      plates & glass. I should have warned you
I have the coldest hands. Set up tollbooths
      & salt licks, glue twigs on old ads
for remedies & resorts, last resorts, prop

      a mermaid in a canoe, & place a gourd in her
prophetic hand. Crushing in both senses.
      Keep this in mind & go easy on me.
Let the bartender skewer the passionfruit,
      envision nudes in tangled roots, & cross

your fingers this volcano spews no more
      than a few euphemisms for love or war.
If all else fails, park a Chevy at the edge of
      town & spread a pelt on its steel roof,
choose the constellation you'd imagine if we

were looking up, languid with disdain
for the rest of a world we know will never live up
to the wistful ersatz aftermath of this.

"In case of emergency, break everything"

jealousy / *jalousie*

As a jealous lover, I suffer four times over: because I am jealous, because I blame myself for being so, because I fear that my jealousy will wound the other, because I allow myself to be subject to a banality. I suffer from being excluded, from being aggressive, from being crazy, and from being common.

EVE is colloquial, sensual, flip. Exasperated, flushed, hair disarrayed, she limps on one bare foot and one high-heeled shoe, which at some point she removes.

ADAM is formal, meditative, aloof. He is dressed in creased trousers and polished shoes, and bears some single sign of trauma, such as a Band-Aid on his forehead.

SETTING: The couple awaits rescue in the wreck of their marriage. In the center of the stage is a crashed Cessna, spray-painted gold, filled with and surrounded by debris, signage, broken furniture, dolls, other toys and household objects, and dirt.

At intervals throughout the scene, EVE bends down and brushes a bit of potting soil from the stage floor into her hand, as if trying, ineffectually, to clean up the mess. She has no broom, only her hands. Each time she sweeps up a handful of dirt, ADAM holds out his open palm, and she drops the dirt into it. When she moves on to another spot, he discreetly turns and deposits the handful of dirt somewhere else.

EVE

He's dead.

ADAM

He is in a condition of perpetual departure, of journeying. He is, by vocation, migrant, fugitive.

EVE

He's *dead*.

ADAM

He created meaning out of nothing, and it was meaning which thrilled him: he was in the crucible of meaning (*gestures toward the plane*), caught, stuffed into a role.

EVE

Into a sack.

ADAM
(*rapidly*)

The lover's discourse is an extreme solitude. Once a discourse is thus driven by its own momentum into the backwater of the unreal, it becomes the site, however exiguous, of an affirmation.

EVE

I don't know what you're talking about.

ADAM

You know perfectly well.

EVE

All I know is we're wrecked, torched, fucked, stuck in the nosedive of us, the newspapered outhouse of us, the splintered dinette of us, the smoke-smudged door of us.

ADAM

The floor of us.

EVE

How can you just stand there with your infernal composure? Decompose! How can you to leave a woman hanging there (*indicates a headless Barbie*)? Tear gas! News flash! Freezer burn! Fear in the form of ice cubes—clink clink.

ADAM

The lover emotes and reposes, wields tyranny and tenderness. Legal tender.

EVE

He adored me, implored me. He was Malibu classic, old-school Mickey whistling on the steamboat, a beech that keeps its leaves till the last.

ADAM

Lucky you.

EVE

Lucky Strike, Lucky Charms. Did that hurt?

ADAM

Some.

EVE

Do you want me to try harder? Where does it hurt most? Your landing gear? Your snowman shrine? Your bear in a body cast?

ADAM

I should like this map of moral acupuncture to be distributed preventively to my new acquaintances.

EVE

You knew full well. When we were cruising over the water, you said it yourself: we are breaking up. We were coming in over the water, the late afternoon sun tinting the whole of the fuselage gold. We banked left, and you wished us into a tailspin.

ADAM

We were breaking up.

EVE

And in the last second, that flame from the engine, that light of your pride, swallowed up the wing.

ADAM

And here we are. The lover maneuvers through the image-repertoire, the path behind him strewn with aspersions of blame.

EVE

It's not my fault that bunny's on crutches.

ADAM

I never said it was your fault.

EVE

But you look at me like you think it's my fault, and you never say that it isn't.

ADAM

Maimed, impoverished, stripped of sense and value.

EVE

That's all you ever think about!

ADAM

How do you know what I think about?

EVE

Just look at this place! It's the burned-out husk of backwards
T-A-X. Broken pencils, poker chips, Grecian urns, Looney Tunes,
toilet seats, targets, clowns. All those *HA HA HA*s, all that epoxy!

ADAM

I thought I was thinking about all the things that are your fault.

EVE

Do you know what those are? (*indicating the hanging gold tires*)
Our rings. Our bloated, galvanized, threadbare wedding rings. Our
nooses, our gallows, our pillory, our stocks. Our once-upon-a-time
in the back of a Plymouth sedan, coming up for air smelling like
gasoline and cheap perfume, checking our faces in the rearview.
Do you remember? Do you remember what it was like?

ADAM

I do.

EVE

We were getting laid in the 70s.

ADAM

We were born in the 70s.

EVE

Tell me, since we're stuck in this hangar, what happened to the
three of spades?

ADAM

(*shrugs*)
What happened to Mosaic law?

EVE

What happened to the bathroom sink?

ADAM

What happened to the Fiat Lux?

EVE

What happened to the fucking chairs?

ADAM

Did you think I wouldn't notice the snake, the writing on the wall?

EVE

Do you answer every question with a question?

ADAM

Does that bother you?

EVE
(*pushing past him, indignant*)

Do you mind?

ADAM

I mind.

(*They stew in silence, circling the plane. EVE stops
at the radio nailed to the tree.*)

EVE

Wait, do you hear anything?

(*ADAM comes to her and pauses, listening to the
static, then shakes his head.*)

ADAM

He's not coming back for you.

EVE

Obviously (*gesturing toward the plane cabin*), but do you hear anything?

ADAM

(*pausing, then shaking his head*)

No signal. No words for the lost in a sea of words, a landfill of words.

EVE

Words? The only words you know have *vag* in them, like *savage*. Stop and look at me! There's nothing left to break. There's ash and splinters, scrap and trash. There's nowhere to sit.

ADAM

(*turning back toward her, crisply*)

Not the shimmy but the shim.

EVE

It was a *nightstand*. One nightstand. One night stand. One. Night. Stand. Don't walk away from me! Every chair is shattered, every rung smashed, every broom snapped over a knee. Pull the drawers from their runners, the hinges from the jambs! Pry the floorboards from the joists, the sills from the architrave, the shoulders from the neck! Bend the hardware beyond recognition, batter each rib and flange! How can you just stand there?

ADAM

The art of the catastrophe calms me down.

EVE

(*breathless, then quieter.*)

These are the after-lights, the after-ash when the fuel tank detonates, an incinerated kiss. American Genesis, so long after the fall no one notices. We came in through a nine-light door into the inside of a gun barrel, an incinerated tunnel of after-love.

ADAM

The lover knew. We are our own demons, our own rivals, our own clichés.

EVE
(*weakly, defeated*)
Minute rice. Heat wave. Box cutter.

> (*EVE bends down again to sweep soil into her hand, but this time she sinks to sit against the burned-out wall. ADAM looks down at her. Then, pinching his trousers, he crouches. They wait in silence for several long seconds, facing the plane. She passes him some dirt, which he deposits on his other side.*)

ADAM
(*breaking the silence*)
In the game, there were as many chairs as children, minus one. While the children marched around, a lady pounded on a piano. When she stopped, everyone dashed for a chair and sat down, except the clumsiest, the least brutal, or the unluckiest, who remained standing, stupid, de trop, one too many—the lover. And so.

EVE
You didn't have to go and smash the dollhouse too.

ADAM
Of course I did.

> (*EVE brushes some dirt off her hands into his open palm and stands.*)

ADAM
(*looking up at her*)
Tell me, Eve. What did he understand that I did not understand?

EVE

It's all here. Our fruitless labors, our luckless fruit. Lapsed subscriptions, lapsed desire—in cinders, in shambles, in a smashed guitar. Dracula on a dollar bill. *Jesus, A Boy's Best Friend.* The girl who says she saw her .44 caliber killer. The high-gloss hope of the body shop. And the pieces of pottery that once made the vessel, once held the wine.

(*ADAM stands and goes to her. He smears some dirt on her cheek. They kiss. Lights down.*)

"Built for speed & languor"

languor / *langueur*

In amorous languor, something keeps going away; it is as if desire were nothing but this hemorrhage. Such is amorous fatigue: I am tired of you I want you I dream of you.

Fatigues thrown over a chair, an olive pall
        over a tented interior.
She lies on a mattress in white bulb light,

        holding a toy
airplane just above her breast, pinching
        the slim fuselage

as one holds a pencil, French tips on her nails,
        areolas soft, skin
flushed and wilted despite the fan. Steam rises

        off the macadam outside
after fourteen hours of baking sun. This depicts
        her anxious wit,

writ large on ruddy flesh, her desire
        grasped between her
fingers as a toy airplane, the shadow

        of which crosses her
torso from one teat to the other. She becomes
        this nude, this prop

plane held against her breast, this place
        between the Cape
and Satellite Beach where the retired

        colonels gather
at dusk to complain about the government,
        debate casino laws

and worry their women were right all along
        about shaking
their bad habits. The shadow elongates,

        broadens across
her clavicle, just as an incoming plane
        casts a shadow

on the ground, making her a landscape,
        smudged by thumbs—
charcoal smudge like the smashed wing

        of a moth as big as
a mouse. A crease down the center
        of her pink torso

like a magazine. Relic of the Cold War.
        Move the lamp
a little to the left and it looks like R&R.

Solitude triptych

loneliness / *isolement*

The lover's solitude is not a solitude of person (love confides, speaks, tells itself), it is a solitude of system: I am alone in making a system out of it.

She starts to roll up the newspaper
where he cleaned the fish, wraps

the cartilage and tail in the Sunday
real estate section, scrapes the pile

of iridescent scales and fatty
ribbons into the center, smears

the serif S of the headline, pauses
for a moment to skim the obits—

banker, baker—tightens her grip
on it, this wad of papier-mâché

that spares the surface, spares
her another look at the closed

door, behind which he rests his
eyes, beyond which—the sea

with its blue anthology, no face
in that blue, no face and no door.

*

A woman marries at 20 and moves
with her husband, because the pay

is good, to a lighthouse a half mile
off shore, reachable only by boat. He

keeps the light, she keeps the stove;
he rows out for supplies, libations;

she lights her cigarette off the burner,
makes instant coffee. When the baby

comes, she puts the playpen in the sun
by the rocks, passes daylight hours with

newspaper, needlepoint, clothesline,
vista—the gap between the Palisades

at Nyack, the ongoing, undetectable
erosion. She knows they will fail, will

plan to last the second summer but re-
consider when the baby learns to walk.

*

Minutes cling to the underside of the leaf.
The space is fur-lined, dry-mouthed. She

tries to remember what brought her here,
where the mouth of the river is the mouth

of the sea, where she fingers the day's hem
and a stray thought reminds her of the fire

she saw from the window of a Montreal hotel
the night of the turn of the millennium,

the night everyone expected the world
to end—a fire in a defunct brick factory

on the next block, a fire searing through
the freezing night and flashing red

in ice from the runoff from the hoses
on streets nearby, a fire drawing engines

from all over the city on the night
everyone expected the world to end.

Interior paramour

loquacious / *loquace*

The flux of language through which the subject tirelessly rehashes the effects of a wound.

Alone with you
in my head I keep right on talking,
telling you tales,
letting you listen in while I ramble on
about rodeos, tamarinds,

fallopian wontons, ruminative moods attuned
to uterine conclusions,
as if you have all the time in the world to hear
my confessions, concessions,
to assure me I'm not alone with this wish to

dismiss stichomythia
as symptom—Ignatius Loyola with a lisp, mere
topical apocalyptic
ointment for a wound and a want that aggravate
an itch like a skip

in vinyl on a voluble turntable, my favorite song
stuck on a single phrase,
and why not—*Love makes me think too much.*
My mind is *a machine*
running all by itself, a hurdy-gurdy whose crank

is turned by a staggering
but anonymous bystander, and which is never silent.
I am language-mad:
no one listens to me, but I go on talking
as if you can hear.

Televoracle

medium / *médium* // media / *médias*

Then begins a kind of long insomnia.

Breaking news. This is KVVU Fox 5
reporting live from the Hoover Dam
as ten thousand gather tonight, a tractor-
trailer overturned near the Paradise overpass,
and four women were found in a Henderson
basement, captive in a kitchenette with six
children. Rubbernecking delays inbound.
Police found a girl cowering in the covers
on a cherry four-poster, carved balusters
stretched with a yak's hide: *Voilà*, the bed

is a drum. Go on, beat it with a bobbystick
for those bearded beauties, 5 o'clock shadows
found in good health—a riot in the thalamus,
a fair in *les ovaires*, a nail head that asks you
to name it then smack it with a hammer,
dammit. Client, rustico, jet-setter, John.

Does she rest her cheek on leather or
pleather? Is the hide of an animal cool?
Her fingers find their way into the button-
tufted dimples in the seat, the way a child
kicks her shoes off under the couch. All girls
want to put a few extra holes in themselves.
To hang stuff off. Her peach fuzz cheek,
her wispy bangs, and oh, that elegant foot—

second toe longer than the first, petite girl
for a size 9 shoe. She grew up near a reactor.

Did I mention her impeccable dress—abacus
of blossoms, popcorn strings, errata—the nap
goes only one way, the same way as her zipper-
toothed mind. Do you see how well lit she is?
Under a warming lamp. What leads you to believe
her hands are bound, that she didn't just slump
to the side? She's a moody recruit. She is off
the shoulder. She is, by definition, a daughter.

What happened to her little friend? Look
closer: each tufted button is the long-lashed
eye of the luxury guest—high roller, priority,
preferred, elite, concierge, club. She has
the lashed laugh. She crosses the rainbow-
mushroom-paisley carpet with soundproof
asbestos under-foam. Neighborhood watch:

three youth charged with criminal mischief.
Look around—statutory, statutory, statuary.
Men made these beds; women lie in them,
and about them. True false true false true
false true: she's been crying for an hour
and the hour is getting threadbare, so we
may as well make some music: mirage, pulse,
pulse, adieu. Mirage, pulse, pulse, adieu.

Are you all right? Did you cut yourself?
Do you want me to get somebody?
Hold pressure. Hold for the next available.
Stand by for World News—I'm your chorus,
your orchid-rhymes-with-orange oracle, your
stiletto Geppetto pancetta vendetta latte
hottie reporting live from the mall:

I'm televoracious, televivacious—
your Heat Miser hand sanitizer, in-
patient, outpatient, up-patient, down-
patient dumbwaiter down the hatch.
It's a harp, and I'll harp on it. A bed
is a drum is a loom is a bed is a drum
is a loom is a bed. Back to you, Bob.

Confidant

metaphor / *métaphore*

*No, that is not what your cry means. As a matter of fact, that
cry is still a cry of love: "I want to understand myself, to make
myself understood, make myself known, be embraced; I want
someone to take me with him." That is what your cry means.*

She is *a person of inclosing reserve.*
She is now *a person of inclosing
reserve with one confidant,* telling him

about the trail she often runs along
the old Putnam line, memorable
boulders, kudzu and such, meadows

of high grass except for a swath
the mower cut. She tells him about
the time in college she tried to sew

a dress but came to an impasse
when she meant to attach bodice
to skirt, misaligned the selvages

or pinned it frankly inside out,
so when she revealed the seam
it frayed in her hands, ragged

underside of a horseshoe crab.
Despair is that dialectical,
as sickness is to cure, as any

anecdote at hand is to visceral
memory: the body runs on its
own time while the mind splits,

half woman, half not. For all
her efforts to run away from
heat or flame because to speak

her rage would distort reason
and need, she forgot becalmed
is a bad thing. Stopped dead.

Going nowhere. How did a boat
get in here, when we were talking
about a dress? She thought it

safe to say he and she were cut
from the same cloth, close-knit,
shuttling between want and will,

and now here they are up a creek,
run aground, shaky at the helm,
adrift, three sheets to the wind,

high and dry. *However, it may
happen that just because she has
opened herself to another person*

*she will despair over having done so;
it may seem to her that she might have
held out far, far longer in silence.*

"Ampersand"

metonymy / *métonymie*

The figure refers to the point of contact, one body touching another, proximity.

Corruption of the phrase *and per se and*, four beads on a string—she wants to tell it to his ear, his ear a warm thing, with her mouth, a warm thing, because the thing is a Roman ligature (& your hand), because the thing is a system of shorthand (& your eyes), because the thing is found in graffiti in Pompeii (& your mouth). Saxon and Latin—the Anglo *and*, the clerical *in itself*— as in melon & hill & clavicle & clef. Reversed capital gamma, Carolingian miniscule, later the routine slur recited at the end of the alphabet, the twenty-seventh letter—*and per se and*—came to mean rear, hindquarters, ass. His hands on her ass & her mouth at his ear, his mouth & ear & melon & mouth & ear.

Mrs. Shandy

Mrs. / *Mme*

"She's not mentioned in the book enough for her to be the
subject of your term paper."

We know only that she is the truest
of all the Poco-curantes of her sex—

in other words, she doesn't give a shit.
She *would go on using a hard word*

twenty years together—and replying to it
too, if it was a verb, in all its moods and

tenses, without giving herself any
trouble to enquire about it. Dumb

blonde: *he was not able for his soul*
to make her comprehend the drift of it.

She yeses him. Until she doesn't.
She won't have this baby without

the midwife, won't prop her legs
in the stirrups for that obstetrical

quack. He tries to reason with her,
tries commotion, harangue, bluster,

but *she had the advantage of a small*
reinforcement of chagrin personal

at the bottom which bore her up.
Chagrin personal in the parlor.

He loses his shit—*for a man to be*
master of one of the finest chains

of reasoning in nature,—and have
a wife at the same time with such

a head-piece, that he cannot hang up
a single inference within side of it.

Vegetal existence at Shandy Hall.
She knew no more than her backside

what he meant. Nose to nose, forceps
to sash, he is obsessed with penises'

potential for generating, if nothing else,
anecdotes. "To have a green gown"

means to get it on: *her whole wardrobe*
followed . . . her red damask,—her orange

tawney,—her white and yellow lute-strings,—
which is the wrong end of a woman?

Susannah, that leaky vessel, cannot
remember the four-syllable name

Trismegistus long enough to get it
to the baptismal chamber, let alone

the widow Wadman's pudenda.
She exerts her influence in the space

of a pause—capacity to eavesdrop
and referee. Which spouse makes

the stronger case? She won't have
that buffoon at the birth, she won't:

*blankness and opacity at its most
eloquent.* Chagrin personal, mute.

Her name, Elizabeth Mollineaux,
appears only in the marriage articles.

River Graces at the mooring

novice / novice

She asks the other women how to swim in open water.

EUPHROSYNE

When you are ready,
wade in. Expect a jolt,
a shudder, when your body

immerses, when you transpose
from land to water creature,
which you once were.

THALIA

glade
rudder
blur

AGLAIA

There is heat in your veins but your heart is still weak. Leave the
cove. Every few strokes, pick up your head to spot a point on
land—a bulkhead, a flagpole, an outcropping of trees. Sight is a
verb, a rhythmic motion. Sight.

THALIA

Vastness comes on fast.
You are a fleck under that sky,
a white swim cap, a whitecap.

EUPHROSYNE

Some days there is chop,

rough currents that pull
with or against the wind.

Or wind from the north
and a strong north-pulling
tide. Keep your head down:

your own forward motion
will make a pocket of air—
slip through the swells.

THALIA

slough
rescind
aside

AGLAIA

Mahican: *muhheakantuck*, the river that flows two ways. Effluvial
and tidal, and both at once. No more or less complicated than
your heart, with its systole and diastole, its loyalty and wanderlust.
Almost an estuary. Almost a sea change.

THALIA

You will come to know the river
as you know a house, as you know
a body, a medium to move through,
a medium that moves you.
You will start to know
that you don't know what to do.
River that flows two ways.

EUPHROSYNE

The river is a room
with walls and roof
unfolded, fallen open.

Four forces: current,
tide, gravity, wind.

THALIA

squall
source
wilt

AGLAIA

Some days it is dirty, the shallows a swill of wood chips and
seaweed. The women still swim. They emerge with brown beards,
wiping their mouths and chins with the backs of their hands. The
women worry about PCBs and pesticides and dredging and sewer
mains, about Albany and industry. But they are getting in, joking
about their limbs fluorescing in their beds, swimming in their
sleep, never reaching the point.

THALIA

On a day when it is too rough to swim,
when the cumulus kicks up a gale,
stand barefoot on the moorings
and read the river surface—
gunmetal, ochre, sea glass, spruce.
Watch all of it go wan, as if the color
were let out a drain in the bottom.
Stand on algaed planks where the paint wears thin,
where the marsh tide wets the edges with detritus.
The river stretches, a tin roof
over the lone room of the world.

EUPHROSYNE

Some days the current
will work against you.
Reach. Turn your body

through its full length—
a long spring of power

with every half-turn,
every core motion, core
tide, countertide.

THALIA

phrase
breach
roil

AGLAIA

Have the sense to stay down, under the churning. There's barely a
breath's worth of air, but you'll find it. Find the fist of air. You know
in your cold bones that none of it is a metaphor for anything.

THALIA

Soon, sooner than you think,
the river will be under ice floes again.
You will wait in the icehouse
for the wind to die down.
The river will keep flowing
but flats of ice will collect in the coves,
and you will stand in the icehouse and watch the surface rip apart.
The icehouse is above you, around you.
Rhombus, rise over run.
Gunwale and domicile.
Trapezoid, trap door.
You are waiting to see
what you are going to do.

EUPHROSYNE

The roof floats off
so the crevice of air

is a door. Floor is
ceiling is roof is wall.

AGLAIA
The river doesn't care what you decide.

THALIA
abreast
asunder
awash

EUPHROSYNE
This is buoyancy.
Bob and crest, reach

and glide, and glide.
If you tire, turn over

on your back, take
a long breath to rise.

THALIA
mire
elide
surmise

AGLAIA
This is the river's rhythm—parallels, striations, arrays. Extension
and crux.

THALIA
This is drift.
Ubiquity.
Ballast.

EUPHROSYNE

The river cleanses itself
twice a day with the tide.

THALIA

belied

AGLAIA

The river cannot clean itself any faster, when it is poisoned. It has
to wait for the moon.

THALIA

When you go home and wring out your confusion,
it is not river water in the basin,
it is confusion.

EUPHROSYNE

You want to swim across,
cover the whole distance,
leave one bank and arrive

on the other, look back
and see the river anew.
You want to be new.

THALIA

resist
shrive
askew

AGLAIA

It is the same river.

THALIA

You can choose not to breathe
for longer than you thought,
but breathe.

EUPHROSYNE

It is a long way across.
You try to carry words
in your head, verse and

stroke, verse by stroke,
but you can't hold
the words, can't hold

a thought. You return
to water and breath,
breath and mouth, water

and mouth. It is a long
way from bank to bank,
across the deep channel.

THALIA

tarry
fraught
blank

AGLAIA

The current is strong in the deep channel.

THALIA

Some fathoms deep.

EUPHROSYNE

Fear is a medium just as
the water is a medium—
translucent, olive, cool.

It is brine in the back
of the throat, a brackish pond.
Fear is a medium

of immersion, perfusion,
but it is outside yourself.
You can swim through it.

THALIA

unspool
supine
confusion

AGLAIA

Go on, swim across.
Go on, swim.

THALIA

Across the deep channel.

EUPHROSYNE

Some fathoms deep.

AGLAIA

River is river.

THALIA

Fear is fear.

                    EUPHROSYNE

Water and mouth.

                    EUPHROSYNE, AGLAIA

Breath and mouth.

                    EUPHROSYNE, AGLAIA, THALIA

Water and breath.

Venus de Milo with drawers

offspring / *progéniture*

Historical reversal: it is no longer the sexual which is indecent,
it is the sentimental.

(forehead)

spoon
watercolors
lavender
the question "What's in your grandmother's drawers?"
sensation of reaching for metal knob and touching mink

(left breast)

straight pin
rosary
year of grandmother's birth, 1921, etched in plaster
peanut butter cookies pressed with a fork when the dough is raw
praise
# # # # # # # # # #

(right breast)

pillbox
photograph of grandmother at 29 in skirted bathing suit with
    Roxanne daisies
unperforated coupons
theodicy

cinders
Sacred Heart nightlight
toothache

(rib cage)

receipts
pewter
Palm Sunday palms
fig
tremor

(abdomen)

egg timer
turpentine
complacency
starlings

(knee)

shears
South of the Border refrigerator magnet
Jones Beach, 1963, her handwriting on the back
Prayer of St. Francis of Assisi
lassitude
salt

Phallophilia

phallophilia / *phallophilie*

The figure refers to the figure refers to the figure.

You once found this hard
to believe but soon enough
you knew you wanted it

in your mouth. One day
your mother will read this
and you will take a sip

of espresso and think about
how you really should cut
your cuticles. The rest of

the poem goes like this:
the first hot day in May
there's already sick-sweet

boy funk in the subway
mixed with piss. Come
up the steps into blooms

all over the gum-blotched
sidewalk—it's ailanthus
you're smelling, behind

the commons gate. Tree
of heaven, invasive frond,
home to moths that make

a cheaper silk. Slake
is the word you want
under your tongue.

You're not dreaming of
anything. That's just what it
smells like—semen, soap.

Twombly's Leda

rape culture / *culture du viol*

The girl isn't sure what he means by ravishing.

How haphazard god is, thrashing about
in teen graffiti, doodling the loopy boobs
he likes to look at amidst the scribble

-scrabble and curlicue pigtails, a few
mustard smears, red-tinted buttercream
for lips and hearts. This is an explosion

evoked by an almost-dried-out magic
marker. This is a joke—a drawing of
a lightbulb or a woman bending over,

a filament or the crease of her ass.
This is the paper after the frustrated boy
erases it over and over, then reaches,

bored, for pink chalk—almost time
for a tantrum. This is the sulfur phallus
& the ampersand. This is rape, people.

His careless power. Haste, thrust, one
golden moment when the coils seem like
they could become something—a spring,

or a flank of springs, winding into
a metallic system of tensile strength.
But it peters out. It was a stupid idea.

At least the etchings on the cave wall
are now etched inside her head, and
that drip of encaustic, that's cum

on her thigh, of course it is. He wipes
his filthy hands on her dress, looks
around at the mess: would someone

please get in here and clean this up?
The great god Jupiter draws himself
one tidy window and climbs out.

Thérèse on a bench

regard / *considérer* // regard / *estime*

I am like those children who take a clock apart in order to find out what time is.

For a few bars of birdsong, she is rapt, her face ablaze
with shame, bliss—with shame-bliss, sham awe—but
her neck where he turned it starts to hurt, the corner

pokes her ribs, her palms moisten and start to slide.
She counts to sixty, squirms, sulks—*growing time that drags
at the knees, time of defenseless waiting.* There. He takes a sip

from his water glass, clears his throat to bring her back
to attention. This is no fun at all. She is hungry. She is
left out to thaw, to pull herself together, a mien hewn

from limestone, a mud-flecked expanse where anger
seeps through wet wool, a poker face. She could be
Jeannette Aldry, Georgette Coslin, Laurence Bataille,

Odile Bugnon, Frédérique Tison, Thérèse Blanchard.
Some girls like to rub up against things—roll arm sofa,
alder. Nothing awakens (because it was never asleep).

*

Pull up a chair, a salmon-pink table in the Savoie
where she plays Solitaire, waiting for the adults
to clean up after the war, to round up the *mères folles.*

A cat pushes its paw toward a morsel, an undulating line
from neck to flank to leg to foot with no fewer than four
rounded peaks, all frosted with sickly lemon light from

the east-facing casement, a Vermeer left out to sour.
She should have a chaperone. His attention is unseem-
ly—it *unseams*, pulls apart selvages—misleads her

into thinking it's not a knife, it's merely a hand
mirror, the kind girls keep on their vanities. He arranges
her ankles *as candidly as when she bites into a pear*, but

it's the panties—the problem is the panties, the smear
that could be shadow or soil. She is only a few months past
menarche, just learning how to savor the onset of pain,

*

the ache and swell as cogs begin to turn, detecting
wetness. Later, long after she has left 3 Cour de Rohan,
she will wait this way for labor, for twinges to build

and get on with it, for pain to blur the Pears' Soap ad
into abstraction and flay her straight from sternum to clit.
For now, for the rest of the session, she lies somewhere

on the spectrum between girl and *his girl*, begins to nod—
I know what I said—you still can't touch her—to nod off,
then remembers—throws down her hand to catch herself

from falling off the bench. The moisture there could throw
any piano out of tune, any perception into a pentimento:
pewter pitcher instead of a footed silver bowl, another girl's

right arm moved to the left while she languishes, reading,
reciting the qualities (brusque, lithe, dour, blunt, carious,
droll), articles (bistro, predation, ginger cat, sommelier),

*

acts (defy, deny, decry). The final hour she can't stand it
a minute more. Nothing amusing is left in her mind, not
one nasty thought or revenge plot. She hates her mother

for saying half-a-hair-past-a-freckle-eastern-elbow-time
and her mother is not even there. Nothing curls right up
under her ribs, stirring her entrails with the silky flick

of its tail—dwelling, *demeure*, a subtle state of amorous
desire, experienced in its dearth, so she shifts her weight,
unclenches her jaw, yawns a big-dog-forepaw yawn—

closes her eyes while he adjusts the shades to let in more
air, less light. Wait awhile, single file. She sees the dark
arrange itself in boxes, follows shadows into nooks, cells,

planes nicked with her impatience—Love, it won't be long
now, we are getting close to time—takes a knife to light,
works at it while her mind loosens and clutters, gathers

*

objects on every surface—the interior of a harpsichord,
a longcase clock, an ocean gate. Somewhere a woodpecker
announces an excerpt: nave, architrave, a chapel fixed up

as a honky-tonk Taj Mahal, but the color has been bled,
has seeped into the sand the way blood drains from bodies
of the morning catch, heads sliced with a serrated blade

and tossed to gulls. All black or all white—her mind turned
by bezel, pinion, wheel, interiors divided into rows, discrete
apartments. Her signage, her storefront, her epoch and hour.

He takes his time, so she sets up her own room: unpacks
utensils from crates and lays them in drawers, removes red
cups to catch more sun, pours it over herself, scalding, saves

some in a wide-mouthed jar. A trio of unmatched chairs.
A mattress that will never fit around that turn in the stair.
A garret, a closet door. Love, we are getting close to time.

A small (or large) machine

resistance / *résistance*

She resists making the other pass through a syntax, a predication, a language. She resists being made to pass through a syntax, a predication, a language.

She busies herself making a machine
for resistance: a clothespin catches a line

and a hatchet comes down, soundless,
onto the pillow, but she flinches, feels a

need for cliché like a need for cake frosting,
decides meanwhile to build a tripod from

limbs of crepe myrtle, jack pine, bubinga,
pushes the pedal forward a half-turn.

She is suspicious of severe goddesses
of the late Victorian sort, shuns sherbet-

toned Medusas, effervescent tentacles
and yolk. No, not yet: she places a moth

on each saucer, runs copper wire through
aluminum cylinders, splices circuits

so the butter knife bolted to a rotary
motor clinks a goblet with each pass.

That will do for now. If she can touch it,
it's kitsch; if she can hear it, it's dreck.

She stashes regret behind a breakfront,
but he sees her do it, pretends he only

recommends the amethyst oysters, leans
across her lap to douse the light again.

Seaside

romantic / romantique

Getaway, getaway car, get away with it.

Have a baby with me, call her Cordelia.
We could linger at the shore, wander

down the boards or along the shoals of
Corson's Inlet, collect driftwood, keep house

in an ever damp bungalow with useless
screens and striped awnings, where surely

we could weather contingency, sun rashes,
pink infernos, console ourselves with oysters,

start to say the same things. Come shoreward
with me, climb a spiral stair to a deck where

we can take each tropical storm by storm,
arm in arm, one moon to the next, until

some balmy August eve when we decide
to venture out to ride the Ferris wheel,

the surf beneath that moonlight stripe.
We'd wake the baby, drive downtown,

rejoice in an auspicious parking spot,
stand in line for tickets in the techno funk,

while human pinwheels swing above us
from metal claws, flung with the force

of a trash compactor, slowed with
hydraulic hiss. The gondolas empty

and fill. We and everyone else in line
will get tired and try to forget we will die

surrounded by plastic, ballpoint
pens, the whir of condensers, waft

of antimicrobial washes. That's salt air.
That's sodium laureth sulfate. Cordelia

Laureth, do you like the ring? How about
Miranda? Do you see the disheveled stars,

the moon over refurbished dunes, over
the sea? Miranda walks onto the sand.

Running out

running / *courir*

"You run ahead? Are you doing it as a shepherd? Or as an
exception? A third case would be the fugitive."

By dark she runs out
of patience with his stories, runs out

into the un-conditioned air
without a word. She'd know
this state with her eyes closed:
the hum of condensers, ocean
and pheromone, spore, sulfur
in the water supply. She runs out

the coastal road at a steady clip,
crosses streets named for lesser
Presidents—Harding, Arthur,
Fillmore, Taft—past the pier, past
a half-built motel, cinderblock
bungalows with louvers to block
the heat of day, clotheslines run out

to the telephone poles across
pebble gardens, hibiscus and
palmetto, imported palms, or-
namental grasses with tassels
in the median. She steps off
the curb when the sidewalk runs out

at Brisa del Mar, a complex
of two-story timeshares some
entrepreneur runs out of his
Orlando office to bankroll
a recording studio for the son.
Flatter-than-flat Floridian
treadmill, Tomorrowland
peoplemover: dog walkers
at this hour. She should turn
back before she runs out

of time to stop at the Quick-
Mart with the cupola and vinyl
facsimile of Spanish tile, but she
wants to keep running in spite
of the time. She wants to keep
running in spite, because no one should run out

on a person they love like this,
because the road ends where the land runs out

at Port Canaveral, just across
the water from the launching
pads at Cape Kennedy, because
the manned space program has run out

of funding. Because defense
contracts. Because off shore.
Because it's bad to run out

of gas on the Everglades Highway.
Because gators. Because Gatorade.
Because the brain will run out

of oxygen in four to six minutes.
Because her grandfather watched
the Challenger explode from his porch,
sitting on his exercise bike listening
to the launch on the radio. Because
night launches were the best—
a blaze at the start, then two flares
when the rocket boosters ran out

of fuel and broke away.

Steingraft

sever / *rompre*

In which she breaks it off.

The wound in the decision.
I have hurt you and you are

as blue as every bit of blue
is precocious. Exhibit A:

seal and matches and swan
and ivy and suit. I am guilty

as charged: a star glide, a single
frantic sullenness, a financial

grass greediness. What's the use
of violent kinds of delightfulness

if there's no pleasure in not getting
tired of it? Don't answer: lilies

are lily white and they exhaust
noise and distance and even dust.

Yes, water makes meadows stroke.
Yes, red weakens an hour. Little

called anything shows shudders.
Exhibit B: elegant use of foliage

and grace and a piece of white
cloth and oil. Exhibit C: not hull

or house, not pea soup, no bill no
care, no precise pearl past pearl

past pearl. The sorrow that came
in. I don't have to tell you this.

The sudden spool is the wound
in the decision. Full stop.

"Slut"

slut / *salope*

What echoes in me is what I learn with my body: . . . the word, the image, the thought function like a whiplash.

Nine muses: tart, slag, slapper, sket, scrubber, trollop, sloven, slattern, hornbag.

Three graces: slut, whore, bitch.

Sapphograft

solitary / *esseulée*

Language is a skin: I rub my language against the other. It is as if I had words instead of fingers, or fingers at the tip of my words.

Believe me, I prayed that night
might be doubled for us. (Thin

flame under my skin.) We know
this much—this parting must be

endured, though I go unwillingly.
Use your soft hands to tear off

dill shoots. Apple branch, wild
hyacinth, greenwood, clover,

thyme. I have a small daughter.
A quince-apple. A girl track star.

Last night I dreamed we had
words. You know the place,

sacred precincts. We quarreled
about my two minds, my child-

like heart. Desire darts, drawn
in circling flight—Andromeda.

Frankly I wish I were dead. Day
in, day out, I hunger and struggle.

Don't, I beg you. Use your soft
hands to tear off dill, crocus.

Remember (you know well)
whom you leave shackled

by love. The night is half gone;
youth goes; I am in bed alone.

Letters on Cézanne

still life / *nature morte*

"Obstacle qui excite l'ardeur"

Are you there, *secretly listening in your eye's interior,*
      alone with his bathers in their frank repose,
their relay of ecstatic arms, the mossy bank, the heat?

      I cannot bear to think of you alone with air
in tones of flesh, alone with his nudes, his ferns
      and clay, as I am alone in woods, ferns, clay.

The still lifes are the most like love, the oils where
      he lays his apples on bed covers, counterpanes,
forms that seem about to roll, but still I cannot bear

      that all your eye will hold are apples in folds
of cloth, apples that are not flesh, folds that are not cloth,
      as if *all of reality were on his side: in this dense quilted blue,*

in his red and shadowless green—an affair settled among the colors
      themselves. So I send you words, skeins of them,
draw yours to me as I would take your face in my hands,

      words I try to touch before they have a chance to cool,
subside, fade. In this way words are like flesh, which recedes
      into indifference—even a lover's hand, left motionless

long enough on the small of the back, a thumb in the hollow
      of a clavicle, ceases to be felt. This is the nature
of touch. Even your touch, as we walked down a dark street

in pseudo-spring, *becomes irretrievable in my memory*
as a figure with many digits. And yet I memorized it, number
        by number. Even in my sleep, my blood describes it

within me, but the naming of it passes by somewhere outside
        and it is not called in. I want to go to you there.
To rest within your solitude without breaking it, this interval

        between parentheses, before it closes. *One lives so badly,*
because one always comes into the present unfinished,
        unable, distracted. We wish it otherwise, *as if*

every place were aware of all the other places, the way he
        has seen it—feverish, humid, furtive—as if we could love
this way, *whole in space, not asking to rest upon anything other*

        than the net of influences and forces in which the stars
feel secure. But I digress. We know we do not want them any less—
        words, touch—because they dim in time,

because we must always lift the object, set it down elsewhere,
        l'obstacle qui excite l'ardeur. Look at this, this place:
a landscape of airy blue, blue sea, red roofs, talking to each other

        in green and very moved in this internal conversation, full
of understanding among one another—moving, moving
        past *rows of trees like a folk song from refrain to refrain.*

Thaw

thaw / *dégel*

Now, no more resonance.

Running along the river road she sees
a chair on an ice floe a few feet off

shore and thinks: a poet would say this
stands for something, but she won't stand

for it, or on it. No shimmer, please—
but shimmer it does, an aluminum patio chair

left on the edge of an upriver cove until
it slid onto the ice, a chunk of which

detached and floated down to the hollow
near the GM site. She runs out of time

and pavement, clatters across the bridge
to the lighthouse, circles and returns.

The chair has drifted in a bit. She could
reach it with a stick. The forecast

calls for thaw, and by the time she
runs this way again, the chair is

gone, or sunk—petty theft, portent.
She knows she promised she wouldn't

make something of it, but cold anger
collects in the fosse of the subdued mood,

spring runoff with poor drainage.
A depression, a hollowed-out place.

"Ugly"

ugly / *laide*

And I, the one who speaks, I too am disfigured: soliloquy makes me into a monster, one huge tongue.

Split at the root: Old Norse *ugga*, to dread or fear; Old Norse *uggligr*, to be dreaded or feared. Frightful, especially through deformity or squalor, intrinsic or extrinsic. Noisome, also nasty, disagreeable, tense: *an ugly mood in the room.* Take that ugly mood outside and whack it with a stick, because it stinks, *pee-yew*, from the Indo-European *pu, to rot or decay.*

Seldom an example that is not a she. First definition, online dictionary: *She thought she was ugly and fat.* 1776: *After having tried in vain to find a wife, even amongst the pert and the ugly.* Maybe if he'd taken off the tricornered hat. Feminized, except for Genesis in Middle English: the *uglike snake.* She dreads, she fears; she is dreaded and feared. The snake is the fulcrum. The snake is the semicolon. An *ugly duckling* shows no sign of the beauty that will come with maturity, but an *ugly American* should shut up about his *French fries.*

It makes an excellent verb. Richardson in *Pamela*: *It is impossible I should love him; for his vices all ugly him over.* All ugly him over! She would have to ugly him over! The film critic said Natalie Portman had to be *uglied up* in *Star Wars*, rendered ridiculous in her Amidala costumery, or her cresting beauty would have swallowed the film whole. She was in an ugly mood, by which we mean she was uncooperative. Morally repugnant, when said of behavior. Stormy, when said of weather, of the sea.

Estrange

uncouple / *désaccoupler*

A turnabout occurs: I seek to disannul it, I force myself to
suffer once again.

We've got to stop meeting like this,
trafficking in cliché over cold chicken and ale,
reeling from the hit-and-run. We're

willfully misinterpreting the text:
though Tom and Daisy, *not unhappy*, sat up late
with the leftovers, *they did not eat.*

Daisy, overwrought, consumed
with fury *for the gorgeous scarcely human orchid*
of a woman who sat in state under

a white plum tree, consumed with
contributary emotion, had no idea she struck down
her husband's lover with such force

her breast ripped from her ribs.
No need to listen for the heart beneath. For our part
we keep on eating as metonymy

moves us to the *crepe myrtles*
that landscape my hometown, preposterous fuchsia,
hussy lilacs. We are inclined

to take a thing too far, even as
we dodge the whole matter of what kind of we we are
pretending to be—the kind where

one of us is turning the pages
and the other, at some temporal remove, stands typing
away at the kitchen counter

(press any key to continue),
a pair onto whose prattling intimacy we may bother
to eavesdrop. We're not the sort

to be deluded by the notion
anyone cares to hang onto our every word. No divas,
we, taking our cold meal of remorse.

"Virgin"

virgin / *vierge*

To love *does not exist in the infinitive.*

A Virgin Mary is a glass of tomato juice. A *virgin* can be a sign of the zodiac, the mother of Jesus, a female insect whose egg can produce a nymph without being fertilized, a variety of apple or pear, a species of moth, or a cigarette made from Virginia tobacco. Virgin, adjective, composed of or consisting of virgins. It takes until definition six to ungender it: a person of either sex in a state of chastity. Virgin bush: not under cultivation. Virgin voyage: first attempt, initial foray. A suite of lexemes, including *virga*, a strip of wood, and *vireo*—green, flourishing, or fresh. Split at the root: she is *fresh*. She is new and unspoiled. She is insubordinate, impertinent, rude. Virgin, when said of wool: not yet, or only once, spun or woven. Said of olive oil: first press. Said of metal: made from ore by smelting. Said of clay: not yet fired.

Losing it

virginity / *virginité*

There is generated in me (a contradiction in terms) a kind of alert fascination: I am nailed to the scene and yet very wide awake.

You have nothing to lose. For decades, across
continents, the elders will say you are losing it—

your innocence, your mind, your temper, your
grip—but here on this fall day, windbreaker

tossed over mountain laurel, shoes off, lying
on your back on pine needles, seeing chandeliers

in the trees while the boy you like fumbles
with his fly, you are nothing if not good, intact.

Trust me on this. Keats didn't die a virgin. Years
later you'll argue this point with a lover, insist

on the likelihood of unreported sex, even if not
with Fanny. Off the record, off the scent, off

a leaf-mulched path behind the elementary school
like any young animal, even one who dies at 25,

choking on mucus, surrounded by bloody rags.
The boy you like will lay his head on your chest,

slide down to the soft belly. It gets chilly. You
reach for your jacket but it won't cover you both.

Inside of an hour

waiting / *attente*

Every musty book becomes a *roman a clef*, each finger put
down on the page an act of divination.

(My Ántonia)

Who knew she only had to close her eyes
to be overcome again by that obliterating

strangeness, the dim superstition, the faint
propitiatory intent. Her color still gives her

an air of deep-seated health and ardor, but
she's never shaken the terror of dying that

plagued her youth, when the road ran about
like a wild thing all the time trying to deny

its error from the surveyed lines, when she
was sure she was being punished for loving

the cold strokes of Chinese white, the two
tawny hawks, the peculiar charms of lying

supine under an oak, the lifting-up of day—
the best days are the first to flee. Leave be-

hind the incommunicable past, so when we
die we become part of something entire,

whether sun or air. There's clemency in those
soft earth roads, a longing to be dissolved

into something complete and great. Stay.
When it comes, it comes naturally as sleep.

(A Lost Lady)

Who knew her own not-youth would become
a strange and palpable character in the room,

eager as a twist of meadow-grass, or as his lips
compressed, frowning into the fire—flange,

hatchet, ravine, sleigh—the words that formed
the scaffold of their seductions, discernments,

decay. Her pale triangular cheeks, her many-
colored laugh—it pierced the thickest hide. He

had the look of a man who could bite an iron rod
in two with the snap of his jaws. Those women,

whose beauty meant more than it said—was their
brilliancy fed by something coarse and concealed?

When women began to talk about still feeling
young, didn't it mean something had broken?

That's a man's question, but she has asked it.
Spring-loaded, a hidden treachery, a trap.

(The Professor's House)

Who knew the thing that had sidetracked her
through cobbled alleys, through tumble-down

ice houses and the ruins of irrigation mains,
would undo her resolve to remain rootless,

unmoored. She wanted to stay with him.
She saw another horizon, a blue, hazy smear—

Lake Michigan, inland sea of his childhood.
Desire is creation, that ink-black rock.

(Death Comes for the Archbishop)

Who knew he'd sleep so soundly on a night like
this, the landscape strewn with broken tongues

and singletrees, smashed wheels and splintered
axles—trifling matters, teasings. Fray. Fray.

Hanging in the portal, over the dry expanse
of sage brush, mind-forged, a talismanic figure

of his versatile intelligence, a harness, a sign
not of a solitude of atrophy, of negation,

but of perpetual flowering in the middle of
his consciousness; none of his former states

of mind were lost or outgrown. They were all within reach of his hand, all comprehensible.

El Jaleo

withdrawn / *renfermée*

*All the solutions she imagines are internal to the amorous
solution: withdrawal, travel, suicide, it is always the lover
who sequesters herself, goes away, or dies; if she sees herself
sequestered, departed, or dead, what she sees is always a lover:
I order myself to be still in love and to be no longer in love.*

If it is lit at all, this long room,
it is moonlit or lamplit, and partial.

She grieves, this much is clear,
her gown a sailcloth, a shroud.

She is ocean-going. She is almost
as tall as her father. A bitter taste

in her mouth—elegy, not adoration,
the gone keeping step with the going.

The only color anywhere is the red
in other women's robes, while

along the back wall, cold plaster,
men carry out their manipulations,

their yelped breaths. Her lover
has thrown back his head to praise

another desire, not one she's privy to,
not one she wishes to understand.

For her part, she has seen this room,
has no further need to keep her eyes

open. She has, from her vantage,
seen the dark and the ardor in it:

We will die before this is through.
We will die before this is through.

Au revoir in Ivor City

yesterday / *hier*

This can't go on.

Play it backwards, this country song:
you get your girl back, your truck back,
and your dog comes home. I'm still sad
about what happened to that dog.

There are a few things I never told you:
Careless with a propane stove, I almost burned
Gila National Forest to the ground in 1993.
I can't remember if I consented in the back

of that Toyota Corolla, really can't, can't
do more than peel back a corner of that
shame. Some labels are like that, impossible
to get off without gummy residue. Come to

think of it, I can't think of a third thing
I never told you. The fuel splashed over
the funnel into the campground scrub.
Go on, stranger. Save yourself from this fire.

Unfinished fugue

you / *tu*

*I myself cannot (as an enamored subject) construct my love
story to the end: I am its poet (its bard) only for the beginning;
the end, like my own death, belongs to others.*

If I were / you were waiting there
outside the door in a long coat holding
your breath / holding my breath,

if I were / you were ruefully amused,
gathering trinkets in the night air,
moons & Mauberley, Burne-Jones'

boudoir & Delphinus & crocuses, I
would breathe the night air, observe
the row of stars above the roof, mis-

take moonlight for snow cover, snow
for salt, for a dune, a bolt of gauze
drawn across the moon, would know

you were (wish you were) asleep in
a white bed, or is it a white field
in Cézanne? Shaded sum of colors,

as if the eye were / I were / you
were standing on an iron bridge,
were waiting at the door, cold

on your coat on your breath on my
hands / if I were there, this—a blaze
of summer straw, in winter's nick.

"Unzip"

zipper / *fermeture éclair*

This is narrative bliss, the kind which both fulfills and delays knowledge, in a word, restarts it.

Flash closure: she sits on the edge of the bed, twists her arm behind her and unzips the dress herself. When she unzips her mind, one side shows serifs and the other camellias. When she unzips the mind under that, one side reveals quartz, tessellations, tassels, the other opals, hypnosis, moats.

The slide draws the two edges together and meshes the teeth in the grooves. X. Y. Z. P. D. Q. If *zipper* were truly a verb, it would be *purloin*. The world's longest zipper, used in the Houston Astrodome, zipped together synthetic grass. A Singapore radio personality unzipped his pants 204 times in 30 seconds, but the record was soon eclipsed by 11-year-old Eric K. of Illinois. She remembers the brassy tracks of his Levis fly—Barthes says, *the lover botches his castration.* She unzips the long boot, slips her foot out of the suede fold—Barthes says, *the garment being merely the smooth envelope of that coalescent substance out of which the lover's discourse, the lover's tongue, is made.*

Éclair: genius, lightning, mob. When they reach the summit, pine needles scattered on bare rock, she pries the caught fabric from the clasp. *Amorous errantry has its comical side.* Holding it taut with her teeth, she gives it a good yank. *Why is it better to last than to burn?* Once unstuck, it takes her no time at all to shimmy out of it. What happens next? When she gets to the end of the alphabet, she finds she has no use for zeitgeist, Ziploc, zodiac, or zygotes, so she turns back to aphrodisiac, back to alchemy, back to ardor, and awe.

NOTES

Excerpts from Richard Howard's translation of Roland Barthes's *A Lover's Discourse* appear in "In case of emergency, break everything" in the voice of Adam, and throughout this book in epigraphs and other italicized passages. The gender of Barthes's pronoun has been altered in several instances from *he* to *she*. If it is in italics, the epigraph for a poem has been taken from Barthes (sometimes minced or regendered); if it is in quotation marks, it is from another source, indicated in the notes below; if it is plain text, it is my own stage direction. The definition poems quote shamelessly from and quibble with the *Oxford English Dictionary* entries for the word in question.

ardor ("Lyrics") echoes a few words and phrases from Van Morrison's *Astral Weeks* (1968) and Wallace Stevens's "Jasmine's Beautiful Thoughts Underneath the Willow."

botanical ("Local flora") takes its epigraph from Wallace Stevens's "Sunday Morning."

complexion ("Tess") comprises scraps of sentences from Thomas Hardy's *Tess of the D'Urbervilles* (1891).

daughter ("Regarding her daughter regarding a maenad") considers an early Roman marble relief of a dancing maenad, one of the mythical women who were followers of Dionysus.

dream ("Ceilinguistica") looks at Brower Hatcher's *Prophecy of the Ancients*, 1988, cast stone, steel, bronze.

gaze ("Amtrakabashed"): the italicized lines that end the poem quote Simone Weil.

housekeeping ("Hardware"): ". . . the 'I' whose predicate can be 'love' or 'fear' or 'want,' and whose object can be 'someone' or 'nothing' and it won't really matter, because the loveliness is just in that presence, shaped around 'I' like a flame on a wick, emanating itself in grief and guilt and joy and whatever else. But quick, and avid, and resourceful" (Marilynne Robinson).

jealousy ("In case of emergency, break everything") is set in Greg Haberny's *In Case of Emergency Break Everything* (*The Money Pit*), 2012, Cessna in mixed media and debris.

languor ("Built for speed & languor") animates Gerard Haggerty's *Ascension #9*, 2001, Conte crayon on paper.

loneliness ("Solitude triptych") glances at Cate Leach's *Red Anthology*, 2001, oil on board.

medium ("Televoracle") is a monologue at the intersection of Chen Zhen's *Vibratoire*, 1997, bedsteads with yak skin and rope; Antonio Santin's *Yeh*, 1978, oil on canvas; and Jeff Wall's *Rear, 304 E. 25th Ave, May 20, 1:14 and 1:17 pm*, 1997, black and white photograph with inset.

metaphor ("Confidant") incorporates sentences from Søren Kierkegaard, *The Sickness Unto Death* (1849).

Mrs. ("Mrs. Shandy") quotes Lawrence Sterne, *The Life and Opinions of Tristram Shandy* (1759-67). "Blankness and opacity at its most eloquent" is a phrase from a critical essay by Ruth Perry.

novice ("River Graces at the mooring") take place in the foreground of Michael Zelehoski's *Open House*, 2012, assemblage with icehouse.

offspring ("Venus de Milo with drawers") references Salvador Dalí's *Venus de Milo with Drawers*, 1936, plaster with metal and fur.

rape culture ("Twombly's Leda") takes issue with Cy Twombly's *Leda and the Swan*, 1962, oil, pencil, and crayon on canvas.

regard ("Thérèse on a bench") studies several paintings by Balthus, including *The Game of Patience* (1954), *Thérèse Dreaming* (1938), *The Salon I & II* (1941–3, 1942), and *Thérèse on a Bench Seat* (1939). In a 1996 interview, Balthus said, "Everything now is pornographic. . . . I have never made anything pornographic." See also Rilke, "Duration of Childhood": ". . . Love, the possessive, surrounds / the child forever betrayed in secret / and promises him to the future; which is not his own. / . . . / Oh how far it is / from this watched-over creature to everything that will someday / be his wonder or his destruction. / His immature strength / learns cunning among the traps."

resistance ("A small (or large) machine") watches the workings of Christopher Deris and Karoline Schleh's *Bobbery*, 2012, mixed media.

running ("Running out") takes its epigraph from Nietzsche's *Twilight of the Idols* (1888).

sever ("Steingraft"): graft as in *greffe*: solace, poultice; splice and unite. As a slashed trunk is lashed to its not-twin, green to green, to yield new fruit. As the cut weeps sap.

solitary ("Sapphograft"): graft as in *greffon*: as over a burn, as a patch over a place where the skin is irreparable. A piece of tissue taken from somewhere else on the body, or from some other body, which the wounded body may or may not reject.

still life ("Letters on Cézanne") quotes several passages from Rilke's *Letters on Cézanne* (1907) in italics, and takes its epigraph from the motto mentioned in the letter dated 16 September 1907: "I am disposed to that patient waiting, that improvidence, in which the birds surpass us, according to Kierkegaard; the daily work, blindly and willingly performed, in all patience and with the *Obstacle qui excite l'ardeur* as its motto. . . . "

thaw ("Thaw") has a passage from Susan Howe's *Pierce-Arrow* (1999) in its peripheral vision: "The chair I appear to / see does not stand / for anything . . . ."

uncouple ("Estrange") rereads a scene in F. Scott Fitzgerald's *The Great Gatsby* (1925).

waiting ("Inside of an hour") assembles fragments and sentences from Willa Cather's *My Ántonia* (1918), *A Lost Lady* (1923), *The Professor's House* (1925), and *Death Comes for the Archbishop* (1927), respectively.

withdrawn ("El Jaleo") looks at John Singer Sargent's *El Jaleo*, 1882, oil.

you ("Unfinished fugue") ends on a line from Wallace Stevens's "The Auroras of Autumn."

ACKNOWLEDGMENTS

Grateful acknowledgment is made to the editors of the following journals where versions of these poems first appeared:

The Account: "Inside of an hour (A Lost Lady), (Death Comes for the Archbishop)"
Barrow Street: "Virgin," "Boredom"
Blackbird: "Girl," "Finger," "Ugly," "A small (or large) machine"
Ducts: "Amtrakabashed" (as "Self Conscious"), "Crush," "Ceilinguistica" (as "Ceiling"), "Lyrics" (as "Enamor"), "Unfinished fugue"
Hampden-Sydney Poetry Review: "Thérèse on a bench"
Modern Language Studies: Prologue, "Daydream," "Interior paramour," "Ampersand," "Mrs. Shandy," "Unzip"
Posit: "Steingraft," "Sapphograft," "Televoracle"
Stolen Island: "Twombly's Leda," "Local flora"
Tinderbox Poetry Journal: "Phallophilia"

"Running out" and "Thaw" (as "Eye Splice") appeared in *Bearers of Distance: Poems by Runners*, eds. Martin Elwell & Jenn Monroe (Eastern Point Press, 2013).

"In case of emergency, break everything" and "River Graces at the mooring" were produced February 14–16, 2013, in *Words that Paint: The Hudson Valley School in Poetry and Prose*, at the Hudson Valley Center for Contemporary Art in Peekskill, New York, directed by Mara Mills.

Lines from "River Graces at the mooring" were adapted as lyrics for the song "On the Moorings," written and performed by Greg Jacquin, *Hudson River* (2018).

Many modes and measures of love, care, and conversation over many years, from editors, colleagues, friends, and beloveds, made this book possible. Let this colon amplify my gratitude: Molly Sutton Kiefer, Nikkita Cohoon, Joelle Biele, Marianne deSalle Horchler, Patrick Henry, Greg Jacquin, Gregory Donovan, Amy Lemmon, Nicholas Nace, Mara Mills, Sarah Blake, Tyler Mills, Jenny Browne, Camille Guthrie, Jennifer Militello, Susan Lewis, Lorna Blake, Simon Waxman, Bill Waddell, Maureen McLane, Deborah Paredez, Jennifer Franklin, Timothy Donnelly, Stefania Heim, Kathryn Hazelwood, Donna and Peter Fischer, James, Emily, and Lauren Allendorf, Gina DeCaprio Vercesi, John Allendorf.

BK Fischer is the author of the poetry collections *Mutiny Gallery*,
St. Rage's Vault, and *Radioapocrypha*, as well as *Museum Mediations*,
a critical study. She lives in Sleepy Hollow, New York.